The Curiosity Theory

A Path From Conflict To Resolution

Martin Lopez

MARTIN LOPEZ

❖

Realtor, mortgage banker, jazz musician, music producer, husband, proud father, and Curiosity Coach.

Working with his mentor Hayden D.M. Hayden to coach organizations in efficient teamwork "flow", Martin observed curiosity squelching arguments and steering conflict toward productive purpose. A naturally curious person, he began noticing that the same thing happened with colleagues, friends, and his own family. So he began to study conflict resolution, why curiosity had such a positive effect, and how he might harness it at the right moments.

The Curiosity Theory is the result of Martin's exploration. Written in the same humorous, conversational style Martin uses when teaching seminars, the book is a guide to practicing The Curiosity Theory to strengthen your relationships in all aspects of your life. Applied curiosity improves communication and collaboration. It helps teams work together more openly and efficiently. It brings friends, couples and families closer together.

Praise for *The Curiosity Theory*

The Curiosity Theory, by Martin Lopez, is a refreshing, wake-up call on how applied curiosity is the glue that binds business, family and all personal relationships together. Full of powerful insights into effective communication skills, delivered in an engaging, easy to internalize style.

– Denis Waitley, author
"The Psychology of Winning"

The Curiosity Theory provides a positive and productive framework to better manage our personal and professional encounters. Too often, we simply react – without fully understanding a situation or fully grasping potential outcomes. Through an engaging and well-written combination of humor, insights, and wisdom, Martin Lopez has developed a powerful and practical tool to help us lead more purposeful and fulfilling lives.

– Chris Heller, *CEO, Keller Williams Realty*

One of the most exciting aspects of mentoring is seeing your mentee take his (or her) own fork in the road.

Martin Lopez began coaching *Conscious Choosing for Flow* with me [five] years ago. An avid student, he dove deep into studying my program and process. He's joined me in coaching companies and teams big and small. We have been on stage together. He is also technically astute and I look forward to each week as we've logged in to co-produce innumerable online videos together, discussing the many facets of successful team communication.

Throughout, I've noticed Martin's fascination with the nuance and art of conflict resolution. This is an area where the solution seems simple (and it is) until we being human gets in the way. We're emotionally wired to sabotage our own best instincts. Even the best of us do it. I watched Martin theorize, experiment, and practice. I've seen him apply it with his coworkers, friends, and family. Even me.

The book in your hands is Martin's distillation of his observations, ideas, and experiments. Though a thinker, Martin is plain-spoken, which makes his efforts highly accessible. He also has a great sense of humor and humility about himself. You'll notice that in reading where he finds wisdom in his own mistakes as much as his successes.

As much as I enjoy working with Martin, I also look forward to seeing him forge his own path down this avenue. As long as he'll let me, we'll keep working together. And I hope he'll still let me be on the stage when we get to the part about *The Curiosity Theory.*

– Hayden D.M. Hayden
Author, *Conscious Choosing for Flow*

Walt Whitman said "be curious, not judgmental." The quintessential basis of The Curiosity Theory is to discover and cultivate empathy while continuing to live out our humanity. It was meant to create an insatiable hunger for not just understanding people, but emphatically connecting.

Martin conveys curiosity such as a close friend sharing meaningful insights of the pains that came from life. His experiences have brought him understanding for those who seek to be understood, commiseration for the grieving, and desire for those who have found themselves to be indifferent. The Curiosity Theory is a safe platform to begin as you take inventory of your life, pursue happiness, and best of all love.

Linda Kline
— Top Producing Realtor

CONTENTS

ACKNOWLEDGEMENTS

Writing a book—even one as simple as The Curiosity Theory—is never the effort of one individual. I have been blessed to be surrounded by incredible people from whom I've learned the lessons I share here. To my beautiful wife Yvette and wonderful children Jordan & Diego, you are the reason I breathe. To my amazing mother and her undying love, and to my family and friends, thank you for your positive energy and love.

There are also those who helped produce, review, critique and refine the text. Thank you so much Casey Delorme and Lori Petchauer, without you I would still be a man with only an idea.

To each of you, may we always remain curious.

Martin

CHAPTER 1

ACCIDENTAL CURIOSITY

Have you ever got out of a fight by accident?

Let's face it, engaging in any form of meaningful relationship we risk conflict. No matter how much we respect or care about people, we're going to occasionally find ourselves at odds with them. Our views differ. Our needs differ. We handle our emotions in completely different ways. Eventually we fight.

Everyone knows the relief we feel when that conflict ends. Doesn't matter if it's a friend, family member, or a colleague. That point where the fight is over and the fire subsides, every part of our bodies releases the tension. You no longer feel the need to fight or run away so you can talk again. It's like the world shifted.

That post-conflict peace is so good that I wanted to figure out how to get there faster. Even better, I wanted a way to avoid the conflict altogether. So I began reflecting on how I get OUT of fights. I discovered an interesting category of fights that ended by accident.

You read right: by accident.

ACCIDENT #1: JUNIOR HIGH

The first incident happened when I was in junior high. Though smaller, Mark was an aspiring Bruce lee. He liked to fight. John, whom we nicknamed Thor for his sheer size, was slow to anger and just as slow to cool off. The three of us were inseparable, always hanging out at lunch and after school.

One day I walked into the lunch room to discover that ring of kids that always gathers to egg on a fight.

"Cool, a fight!" thought my inner voyeur.

But my youthful intrigue ended fast when I saw John throw (and Mark dodge) the first punch. I had no idea what it was about. John often teased Mark relentlessly just to see if he could upset him. Perhaps he had gone too far

As their friend, it was instinct to break things up. I jumped between them more out of not thinking than bravery. I tried to push them away from each other.

"Guys! Guys!" I shouted. "Stop!" (Along with some language I can't repeat in mixed company.)

It distracted Mark enough that he backed off, however, I was now in Johns danger zone. His stare turned my way. His nostrils flared, his eyes narrowed, and his right arm cocked for the punch. I backed away, half-bracing for the inevitable first blow.

People in peril claim to see their life flash before their eyes. In this moment all I could see was John's oversized fist, which seemed big enough to block out the sun. I grew up in a tough neighborhood where even the good kids ended up scuffling occasionally, so I could already feel the damage that fist was going to do.

I sensed three options:

Go ballistic on him. Fists flailing. He would still crush me, but I could maybe get a decent punch or two in so there was a chance of survival.

Make a break for the nearest door. I could even see the red exit sign glowing just over his shoulder.

Freeze. Some instinct thought maybe he wouldn't see me. Like Tyrannosaurus Rex in the movie Jurassic Park. Just. Don't. Move.

As all this flashed in my mind, a singular thought escaped to become words:

"Why... John, why are WE fighting?" I asked.

His expression shifted as though I'd woken him. He tilted his head like a puzzled dog. His arm relaxed. (Whew!)

"I don't know," he said.

It was over that easily. We went through the lunch line once again the best of friends. No hint of the tension remained.

ACCIDENT #2: HECTOR AND SYLVIA

I spent much of my 20s and 30s selling houses in Southern California. I prided myself on congratulating new homebuyers by making an event of giving them their keys. I also made a point of asking for referrals. That was how you continued building your clientele.

Hector and Sylvia were newlyweds buying their first house. We had considered nine or ten other properties before finding the one that fit their dreams and budget. I had arrived early to open the shades to let the brilliant afternoon light into the small, three-bedroom house. In addition, I brought a bottle of champagne, three glasses, and a ribbon for the key.

I heard them coming up the driveway, so before they reached the door, I opened it, grinning.

"Welcome home!" I announced.

Hector shook my hand, grinning with me. Sylvia, however, shot me a frosty look. (Yikes!) Perhaps they had a tiff on the way over. I puzzled over this even as I poured the champagne, let them inspect the property, and arranged final paperwork for signatures.

She seemed to have relaxed by the time they finished signing. I took a moment to trade the pen for a small stack of business cards I kept in my jacket pocket.

"You guys seem happy," I said, smiling my most confident smile. "I think you know that my business depends on referrals from happy clients. Might I ask that, if you are pleased..."

Sylvia held her hand up to cut me off.

"We won't be referring anyone to you," she said, cold enough to re-chill the champagne.

Stunned. I had no idea what to do. I may have dropped the business cards.

"Sweetie," Hector said.

Silence.

"Is something bothering you?" he asked.

She crossed her arms.

"It's my first house. From the moment we made the offer, all I've been able to think of is turning the key to open MY door. This house was already open," she said.

Tears welled. But she'd said what she needed to.

As far as I'm concerned, Hector was an artist the way he asked that question. Rather than prolong her upset, he got right to the heart of the matter, and listened.

We fixed the situation by going outside, re-locking the door, and giving her the honors. I even offered to get another bottle of champagne and a new set of papers for them to sign.

"No," she said. "That's what I really wanted."

They remain friends and have sent me numerous referrals over the years.

ACCIDENT #3: THAT'S MY BOY!

I asked my 13-year-old son Jordan to clear our backyard of dog poop prior to our hosting a neighborhood barbeque. With a large backyard, this was one of those chores that occasionally gets neglected. But it's also a detail you really notice before guests arrive. It was his assigned chore, agreed upon when we adopted a puppy.

I reminded him in the most fatherly way possible: Nagging. At 10 a.m. And noon. And 2 p.m.

At 4 p.m. my patience expired. Guests were due any moment. My wife and my other son were busy with finishing touches on hors d'oeuvres. I was cleaning the barbeque when Jordan strolled across the back patio.

"Jordan!" I commanded. "You've had all day to goof off. Pick up the poop. Now."

He looked at me sideways, but grabbed the scoop and plastic grocery bags I'd purposefully placed on the patio for him and got to work.

So did I. Never wait until the last minute to clean a barbeque.

A while later, he passed by me on the way to the trash can.

"Now, was that so hard?" I asked.

He looked at me with the most amazing expression of defiance I had ever seen. Eyes wide. Jaw set. Then he marched to the center of the yard, and dumped the contents of the plastic bag on the ground. He even shook the bag empty. He punctuated this by meeting my eyes and dropping the bag on top of the pile.

I recoiled. My eyes narrowed. I considered chucking the barbeque scraper at him.

As he walked to the patio door, he looked back over his shoulder, then he paused and asked "Dad, are you wondering why I did that?"

My anger gave way to shock. This boy had shown man-level audacity. I wrestled in my thoughts. Was I actually impressed?

"Yes… Yes I am," I said. I felt off-balance, like trying to talk after you've had the wind knocked out of you.

"Mom has had me cleaning all day," he said. "My room, the garage and the TV room. I have not had time to get to the yard. I am old enough to prioritize chores. This one seemed best to do last. Everyone always arrives late and then hangs out in the kitchen for an hour. I thought I could finish the yard after they start arriving and nobody would know. Nagging doesn't make me go faster. It just pisses me off."

"Okay," I said in amazement. My anger was giving way to an even stronger emotion: fatherly pride. Was this articulate kid really my child?

"Now," he said. "I'd like to go to the garage and get a better bag. That's a lot of poop. The bag you gave me won't hold the smell."

CONNECTING THE ACCIDENTS

Those were three completely different situations where conflict flared, but was accidentally avoided. I say accidentally because I was fully engaged to have the inevitable battle, but something short-circuited inevitable. What was that something?

My theory: Curiosity is the common element. It pivoted each moment of conflict into a moment of exploration rather than a fight:

"Why are we fighting?" I asked John. He had to think.

"Is something bothering you?" Hector asked Sylvia, opening the conversation so she could express herself.

"Are you wondering why I did that?" my son asked me, forcing me to admit I was, in fact, wondering.

Working with *The Curiosity Theory*, I began to see that curiosity was a starting point. But it wasn't curiosity alone that transformed the conflict. It was the fact that curiosity signals a desire to truly know.

Why ARE we fighting?

What IS bothering us?

Why DID we do that?

Faced with conflict, our first instinct is reptilian: fight, flight, or freeze. We brace ourselves for what is to come, ready to defend, attack, or run away. From that posture, escalation is inevitable.

Curiosity, however, opens the door a crack. A door to understanding, to communication, that can bring us into alignment and to a/

our human connection.

In these three "accidents", curiosity saved the day. However, nobody consciously made it happen. Each time the curiosity came from a different source.

To explore my theory, I needed a way to "practice" curiosity. I needed to make it happen on command; to override my own reptilian response. I needed to understand more about why curiosity was so powerful and how to approach it in these delicate situations.

I began to explore my own mindfulness during conflict (or near conflict). I sought first to observe my own behavior as well as the others' behavior. What led to the conflict? What diffused or even circumvented the conflict? Through a long process of trial-and-error, I developed a practice I call *The Curiosity Theory*.

The Curiosity Theory is about empathetically listening to others. It is about understanding our own needs both in and out of conflict. It is about hearing others' needs. Furthermore, it is about finding alignment that returns us to productive interaction, allows us to work, build, learn, teach, or just plain love. Conflict disrupts all of those things.

The Curiosity Theory is about being able to make curious accidents happen on purpose.

That idea is what I would like to share with you.

CHAPTER 2

❖

THE FIRST TIME I USED CURIOSITY ON PURPOSE

What does it look like when you intentionally use *The Curiosity Theory*?

Recall a time when you were absolutely in the moment. No matter how difficult the work you were doing, you were focused, moving through the tasks required. You were completely in sync with the work itself, as well as anyone else involved in the work with you. Everything else just faded away.

For some, this would be dancing, cooking, or gardening. For others, this could be sports or closing a sale. I have even had an audience member describe large-scale construction project planning this way.

For me, it is playing saxophone in a jazz band. A band geek since elementary school, I broker mortgages by day and am one quarter of a quartet by night.

I feel my fingers on the keys while I hear my notes weaving with the piano, bass, and drums. I smell the beer being delivered by a beautiful blonde waitress. A couple, at a table nearby, sways to our music, even while immersed in one another.

Like any team, a successful band is a multi-party marriage. Considerations go well beyond getting the right instruments in the room. You need compatible talents, work ethic, and creative visions. You have to get along, especially when the going gets tough. In fact, moments of conflict are often where the real creativity is born. Differences. Challenges.

One night, we reached that point in the song where Patrick, our drummer kept changing the rhythm.

Everything was in a perfect flow; each of us was in sync with each other, taking cues for the handoffs. Everyone had time in the spotlight. Everyone knew when to pull back and let someone else shine.

Then, BOOM!.

That wasn't supposed to be there, I thought.

It was like he'd dropped a stick. It threw me off at first, followed by the keyboards. Our bassist punctuated the change with a note that would have needed censoring were it words.

"Pick it back up at the bridge," I said.

We were back, like rewinding a tape and starting again at your favorite part of the song.

BOOM!

"Pat!" the rest of us shouted, in unison.

He looked baffled.

"Why aren't you following?" he asked.

Now everyone else looked baffled.

"Why do you keep screwing up the beat?" Confronted Adam, our keyboard player.

"Why can't you follow me?" Patrick defended.

"That's not how the song goes," Adam said.

Patrick braced for the inevitable argument. He crossed his arms and sat up in his chair. The hi-hat cymbals crashed when his foot left the pedal.

Tense silence.

Then, for the first time, I realized my opportunity.

Patrick's playing BOOMed at the same place every time, exactly the same way every time. Then, the rest of the band quit playing.

Those were the facts.

Everything else—including Adam implying that Patrick didn't know how to play the song—was a story.

I tried to keep my voice as relaxed and empathetic as possible.

"Patrick," I said, interrupting the standoff. "I'm curious. Are you trying to do something on purpose there?"

Braced for a fight, he wasn't expecting someone to hear him. He looked at me puzzled, then wide-eyed, then excited.

"Yes," he said.

He looked to see if each of us was listening.

"We've been looking for a way to get people to leave their seats and dance," he said. "I saw a group do this last week. If we shift tempo right there, it energizes the audience and will get them on their feet."

We all looked at each other.

"Just follow me when I shift," he said. "Let me do a four-measure solo and I'll up the tempo. When you guys drop in, people will dance."

We tried the song again. This time when he went BOOM, it was the attention-getting pop that set off an explosive dance beat. It worked so well, we started dancing right there in my garage.

That weekend at the club, it did the same for the audience. The change was so successful that we held that Friday-night gig for the rest of the summer.

There may be some poetry in the fact that Curiosity kept the band together. Musicians are legendarily emotional types. Bands break up over all kinds of dramas that seem comical to outsiders. The Curiosity Theory helped us move through a difficult moment and work even more collaboratively.

There is an important distinction in what I recognized during that challenging practice session.

FACTS vs. STORIES

It is human nature that, when facing conflict, we allow our emotions to override the facts.

For the most part, creating stories from basic facts helps us navigate our world. It helps us deal with the reality that the facts about anything are incomplete. This tendency to create stories from limited facts probably kept us alive throughout time. Here's how it works: When the forest suddenly goes quiet, we notice and take action to protect ourselves.

Fact: It is dark and quiet.

Story: There's a predator nearby ready to kill and eat us.

Our stories cause us to automatically react and move to safety or prepare to confront the predator. Another automatic reaction is to point a light and scare it off, or grab a weapon we can use to defend ourselves. The end result is the crisis is averted.

But storytelling has a dark side: Our emotion-driven interpretations of the facts are so powerful that we operate as though those interpretations ARE facts. Let's call these assumptions.

Have you ever been accused of something you didn't actually do, but were unable to explain away the facts that made you look guilty? You felt its power.

This human tendency to make assumptions based on a few given facts is so powerful that we derive countless hours of entertainment from murder mysteries, both real and fictional. The same set of facts easily makes several suspects look guilty. The creepy-looking guy's fingerprints were on the knife, so he MUST be guilty. We neglect to ask if there were other reasons his fingerprints got there. Maybe he had to move the knife during his heroic efforts to save the victim's life.

The dark forest: What if everything went quiet because our late-arriving friend finally found the campsite? Our adrenaline is surging. We're in fear, weapons ready to confront whatever pounces out of the darkness. We assumed we were in danger and now we're poised to attack the guy who brought the marshmallows for s'mores.

Back with the band, we had some facts:

FACT: Patrick's playing BOOMed at the same place, the same way, every time.

FACT: The rest of the band quit playing when this happened.

INTERPRETATION: Patrick doesn't know how to play the song.

Suddenly, there's a whole flurry of emotions, stories, and accusations. Argument ensues and work stops.

A single Curious Question allowed us to open the topic, get back on track, and discover Patrick wasn't failing us. He was taking us in a brilliant new direction.

Looking back to my three examples from Chapter 1, what facts do we actually know?

Fact 1: My friends Mark and John were facing each other. I stepped between them and pushed them apart.

Fact 2: Sylvia said she would not refer other clients to me.

Fact 3: My son Jordan dumped a bag of dog poop in the middle of the yard after he had already picked it all up. (I'll also accept the fact that I was nagging him.)

Fact-wise, that's all I (and you, the reader) knew.

However, based on those facts, we can create all kinds of plausible stories. In fact, here are ten great alternative stories:

1. Mark had kissed John's girlfriend at a party the previous night.

2. John had fought with his dad in the morning. John was paying it forward.

3. John got a F in one of his classes and it was because Mark always talks to him.

4. Sylvia hates salespeople.

5. Sylvia thought I dressed badly and didn't want anyone else to know she had associated with me.

6. Sylvia doesn't trust anyone of Hispanic descent. Hector's faith in me was the only reason she'd put up with me in the first place.

7. Sylvia and Hector are very religious and she was upset that I'd provided alcohol.

8. Jordan is an angry child and this is regular interaction between us.

9. Jordan was pranking me, hoping to capture my most shocked look for a YouTube video contest.

10. Jordan is a budding environmentalist and doesn't believe that plastic bags belong in the trash. He was looking for a more environmentally-friendly way to dispose of the poop.

In the absence of additional factual information, we create all kinds of stories. Some stories are ugly, some are comical, and still others are downright ridiculous. But they all appeal to our emotions, therefore, we often operate on the stories rather than the facts themselves.

Practicing Curiosity Theory begins by recognizing that we are:

1. human and, therefore

2. prone to jumping from the facts at the hand to emotion-driven (and often incorrect) stories, then

3. reacting to those stories as though they were, themselves, factual

FACTS VS STORIES - EXERCISE: BABY SHOES

While conducting The Curiosity Theory seminars, we love to practice separating facts from stories using "micro-stories". The concept comes from an Ernest Hemmingway myth. This brilliant American novelist was challenged to a bar bet: Could he tell a story in seven words?

He responded with: "For sale: Baby Shoes. Never used."

In six words, he yanked us straight into powerful emotions. We want to know the details: What happened to the child? Did he/she die? What of? Illness? An accident? Were the parents devastated? Were they guilty?

Or, on the practical side:
Were the shoes the wrong size?
Did mom just find them hideously ugly?
Were they a gift from the evil stepmother?
Were they stolen by a thief hoping to make a buck?

We could spend all day coming up with stories. Our ability to create stories from facts is instinctual and amazing. Some of them would make brilliant movie plots.

Most of these stories assume something happened to a baby. It takes most of us a few moments to draw back to the facts:

1. There are some baby shoes.

2. They are unused.

3. They are for sale.

A baby isn't among the facts. Nor is a mother or father. In fact, there are no characters in Hemmingway's six-word novel.

So, I challenge you to a fun learning game to play with friends.

Given the following micro-stories, answer:

A) How many stories can you create based on what happened?

(Do this part first; it is wildly entertaining AND makes the next part more challenging.)

B) What are the facts?

1. A woman and a man are speaking animatedly inside of a car across the street. They are turned toward each other and gesturing emphatically. She appears to be crying.

   Story: _____

   Facts:_____

2. A woman is leading a 10-year-old boy jaywalking across a busy downtown street. The child is pulling back against the woman's grasp.

   Story: _____

   Facts:_____

3. While folding laundry in the bedroom, you hear a crash and a scream in the kitchen. You enter to find your 10-year-old son staring back at you, a broken jar of pasta sauce, and your 5-year-old girl in tears.

Story: _____

Facts:_____

4. You enter your boyfriend's house to find him packing a suitcase and speaking with a young, attractive woman whom you do not know.

   Story: _____

   Facts:_____

5. Your girlfriend is two hours late for a date. Checking your phone, you see a missed call with the caller ID of a local hospital.

   Story: _____

   Facts:_____

6. Your boyfriend travels often for work. When he calls you, you notice that on several of his calls the caller ID says New Jersey. This is not one of the states he says he travels to.

   Story: _____

   Facts:_____

7. You arrive early for a meeting with your supervisor. On his otherwise organized desk is a post-it note with the hand-written question: What do you do all day?

    Story: _____

    Facts: _____

8. When you enter the small lunch room at the office. Two other employees—one male, one female—noticeably stop talking and look at you.

    Story: _____

    Facts: _____

9. Friends cancel a scheduled night out. You decided to go out by yourself, only to arrive at your neighborhood pub to find several of them at a table together.

    Story: _____

    Facts: _____

10. At 2:30 p.m. on a school day, your 15 year old son leaves you a voice mail stating that he is going to be at the gym until 9 p.m.

    Story: _____

    Facts: _____

CHAPTER 3

❖

USE YOUR WORDS

"Use your words," said my wife, Yvette.

Our son Diego was three. He was at that age when a child is learning to communicate, but still reverts to infant ways when upset. I settled in to watch the mother-child standoff.

Diego took a deep breath, scrunched his face, and started into a full scream. He shoved his sippy-cup across the table. It rolled off the edge and bounced on the floor.

"You can't just scream," Yvette said. "You need to SAY what you need. Use Your Words."

More wailing.

"Are you hurt?" Yvette queried.

Diego shook his head.

"Do you need the potty?" she continued.

"No!" said Diego, emphasizing with a wider head shake. I wondered if his head might swivel right off.

"Are you hungry?" Yvette persisted.

Diego nodded and stopped crying like someone had just flipped a switch to "off".

"Can you say, 'I'm hungry'?" asked Yvette, reaching for a box of Nilla Wafers.

"Hungry!" replied Diego. He giggled and reached for the box.

I laughed, too. Yvette was so strong and patient. We went through the same routine with our older son, Jordan, when he was this age.

I'm sure my mother did the same with me when I was three. I'm certain that you, dear reader, went through the same when you were three and/or have done the same with your own kids.

This is the earliest stage of how we learn "Emotional Intelligence": the ability to be self-aware of needs and feelings so that you can clearly communicate them rather than resort to tantrums. In this chapter and the next, I'll discuss how those needs and feelings extend well beyond the childhood basics of hunger and needing your diaper changed.

The sad part is that most of our formal education in Emotional Intelligence ends once we can say whether we're hungry or not. After that, we're pretty much left to figure it out on our own.

This is one reason why we struggle in the face of conflict, both with our own needs and feelings and with others'. We are stuck within the childhood limits of our own self-awareness.

In Chapter 2, we explored distinguishing between Facts vs. Stories. By identifying the essential tripwires of conflict, we better equip ourselves to recognize and avoid them. Knowing that our interpretations of the facts often get confused with the facts themselves, we are better able to remain calm, separate the two, and employ Curiosity to circumvent conflict and get back to the human connection we desire.

However, there is another critical tripwire. The Reptilian Brain: Something so primal that it fuels on conflict to transform us all into tantrum-prone children. Even those of us who supposedly know how to "use our words" can trip.

AN IMPORTANT ANATOMY LESSON

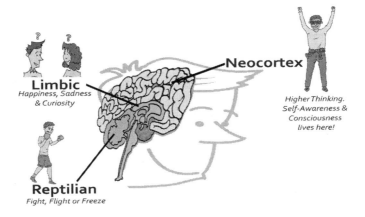

Limbic
Happiness, Sadness & Curiosity

Neocortex

Higher Thinking. Self-Awareness & Consciousness lives here!

Reptilian
Fight, Flight or Freeze

Neuroscientists using advanced brain scanning equipment continue to map the multitude of ways our brain functions as we think and feel.

They theorize that our brain's structure echoes that of the human species' evolution from earlier reptile relatives, through mammalian roots, to the higher-processing components that give humans the largest brains (relative to body size) of any creature living or historical.

At the base of our brain is the brainstem. It is connected to the lower body via the spinal cord and echoes the **Reptile Brain** found in lizards and snakes. Though virtually no thinking happens there, the brain stem keeps us alive by regulating all of the autonomous body systems, such as breathing, blood circulation, digestion, and automatic reflexes. This is the stuff your body does without you ever having to think about it. It is home to our basic emotions of fear, anger, and pleasure.

On top of the Reptilian Brain sits the **Limbic Brain**, which, among other things, processes the more complex emotions, including happiness, sadness, apprehension, and, well, Curiosity.

The **Neocortex** sits on top of the Limbic Brain and makes up the biggest portion of the brain's mass. It houses our higher thinking. It is where our self-awareness and consciousness lives.

Most of the time, our five senses (touch, sight, hearing, taste, and smell) report to the Neocortex, which works in combination with the Limbic System to process the sense data for meaning. This is a mix of thought and emotion. It is where you can differentiate between a car and human being. It connects the visual shape of a human and his/her posture, the sound of someone's voice, the smell of their perfume, and registers that this is your spouse and that you care for him/her.

This allows you to feel affection and respond with a smile, loving words, and an embrace.

However, nestled on each side of the Brain Stem, where it meets the Limbic System, are two almond-size structures called The Amygdala. *Pronounced [uh-mig-duh-luh]

The Amygdala serves as the Reptile Brain's trigger switch. They have a direct pipeline to your senses and are calibrated to recognize basic patterns. Your Higher Brain takes a moment to process the sense information and determine how you actually feel. The Amygdala is set to act instantly if it sees pre-programmed danger. We are talking nanoseconds of reaction time, but that's what it takes to save you. Essentially, the Amygdala can hijack your whole brain to protect you.

Ever "felt a chill" or had the "hair stand up on the back of your neck"? That's your Reptile Brain. Like a startled lizard, you take instant action.

Too close to the edge of cliff? Amygdala backs you away before you feel the fear.

See a snake? Amygdala makes you jump before you know you've seen it.

Remember my earlier example about the forest going eerily silent? Instantly, Amygdala and Reptile Brain get you to:

Fight (or prepare to).

Flight (run away from the danger).

Freeze (hopefully the danger won't see you).

Fight   **Flight**   **Freeze**

These three primitive choices are a major Reptile Brain success. They have kept our Reptile ancestors alive. In its primitive past, Reptile Brain fended off other territorial reptiles, outran hungry saber tooth tigers, and blended into the rock when spied from above by a predatory hawk.

The Reptile Brain's self-preservation instinct necessarily hijacks the higher-thinking parts of our brain. Though this is designed to save lives, it also shuts down our ability to rationalize, think clearly, and communicate. Reptile Brain instantly takes command of our nervous system and blood flow. Adrenaline rushes, heart rate increases, and all five senses—sight, hearing, smell, taste, and touch—become alert and focused.

"Fight, Flight, or Freeze," says Reptile Brain. "Win Now! Talk Another Time!"

Major problem: Reptile Brain senses conflict as imminent danger. Just when we should be listening, connecting, and talking things through with our spouse, child, or coworker, Reptile Brain screams, "Fight, Flight, or Freeze!"

So that's what we do and that's what our spouse, child, or coworker does. This automatic vicious circle derails any chance we have of connecting until everyone's Reptile Brain feels safe and respected. We end up in a futile zone, arguing, fighting, freezing each other out, and damaging relationships. We lose valuable time, ripe opportunities, success and the pleasure of having loved ones close all because Reptile Brain confused conflict with danger.

Fortunately, the Amygdala can be trained. It can learn new dangers, such as a car bearing down on us in the street. (Something our reptilian ancestors never encountered.) It can also un-learn mistaken dangers, such as no more fear of heights for a trapeze artist.

The Curiosity Theory involves training our Reptile Brain to recognize conflict as an opportunity rather than a threat. With practice, our Reptile Brain comes to recognize Curiosity as a path to safety when encountering conflict. It will ease up on the hijacking, allowing Higher Brain to employ our senses and blood flow to a more powerful purpose: Connecting with our spouse, child, or coworkers.

It's not all that different from learning to distinguish between different snakes. Our Reptile Brain makes us jump whenever we see a snake. (It also makes us jump when we see a fake rubber snake and even sometimes when a coiled garden hose does a great snake impersonation.) However, once we learn to distinguish a harmless garter snake from a rattlesnake, we're less prone to instantly jump. Sure, we will still startle, but we recover quickly when our brain sees there is no real danger.

In essence, we can teach our Reptilian Brain to "use our words".

CHAPTER 4

FEELINGS AND NEEDS

"**G**ood night, my love," I said, closing the door of my wife's Nissan Pathfinder.

I watched her taillights as she drove back to the hotel, then I climbed into the tent with our boys for a night of storytelling.

I love camping. As a child I camped all over the incredibly diverse landscape of the Western United States and Mexico. We would pitch a tent on the beach or the high desert. There were mountain forests, grassy plains, and creeks trickling through valleys. I especially loved beach camping, where I could run to the water and boogie board. Then there's that heavenly feeling of sand between your toes.

My wife doesn't exactly feel the same way.

"Martin," she said. "I love the solid feeling of swimming pool tile under MY feet. I love knowing that there's a fresh towel on a chaise lounge within reach. I love a warm shower after, then climbing into cotton sheets instead of mosquito netting."

I do, too. I love camping AND a nice hotel, so I do both. My wife—bless her heart—made an earnest effort to try the camping, but it just didn't agree with her.

However, when our boys were old enough to try camping, we needed a solution that worked for everybody. We love family trips and didn't want to exclude anyone. Those of you in successful long-term marriages will recognize our clever compromise.

It started with back-yard camping. We'd cook on our barbeque, eat at the picnic table, then climb into our tent and tell stories with flashlight shadow puppets on the wall. Everyone got to enjoy the evening together. Once the boys and I fell asleep, Yvette would head inside to our bedroom. She'd often wake us with pancakes in the morning.

As the boys got older, I wanted to show them my own childhood camping locations. But I also wanted to include Yvette. I began researching campground facilities and obsessively carried around an REI catalogue to show her how far outdoor gear technology has come. I mean, there are even solar-powered backpacks/batteries so you're never without your iPod.

She had a better solution.

"Honey," she said, as I showed her yet another tent with a built-in solar-powered dome light. "What if we just found a campground near a hotel? I could stay until bedtime, hop over to the hotel for the night, and come back for breakfast."

It was just crazy enough that it worked perfectly. Sometimes the boys would join her. Mostly they stayed with me in the tent. We all got the joy of camping and I was able to share some of my fondest childhood experiences with my kids. Yvette had her clean sheets and warm shower.

And, as much as I appreciate the romance of making coffee on the campfire, I was thrilled that Yvette would bring us Starbucks when she returned in the morning.

Maybe the camping arrangement is a little odd. Those in successful long-term relationships will recognize doing what it takes to respect the fact that, even (especially?) in marriage, the two of you are still individuals. Though you love doing things together, they may not always be the same things. It takes all kinds of communicating, negotiation, and creative solutions to make it work. This is the real labor of love.

Our camping arrangement illustrates a critical point I want to make in this chapter:

1. We all have basic needs that, even without knowing it, we are inherently driven to satisfy.

2. Our emotions are direct reactions to these needs being met or not met.

Sounds simple; almost like we could just create an equation or even a spreadsheet listing human needs and correlating these to our emotions. Feeling an emotion? Just find it in column A, then read over to column B to see what need isn't being met.

Anyone who has emotions (Read: you and I) will baffle at the idea of them being this simple. The fact that nearly every university has a psychology department teaming with researchers trying to figure out what makes us tick is testament to this topic's complexity. Our needs and feelings challenge even the best minds trying to sort them out. No wonder we confuse stories for facts; not to mention that each of us has that ever-vigilant Reptilian Brain ready to hijack our minds at the slightest hint of danger.

Fortunately, I'm not trying to figure it all out, especially in the context of this book. We can make it accessible by borrowing some well-known psychology theories to inform this practice of using emotions as guideposts to the needs being met or missed at a moment of conflict.

MASLOW'S HEIRARCHY OF ESSENTIAL HUMAN NEEDS

In 1943, social psychologist Abraham Maslow put forth a Hierarchy of Human Needs that his extensive research and cross-cultural observations indicated were common to all human beings. More than 70 years—and countless experiments and other scrutiny later—his Hierarchy still stands.

His theory is diagrammed as a pyramid, with the basic needs (think Reptile Brain; absolutely-cannot-survive-without) as the foundation, and each layer building on the previous. Once a person's base-level needs are met, they become concerned with the next layer of needs (i.e. safety, then love & belonging). Stepping up each level, they eventually reach the pinnacle: Self-Transcendence.

To bring things into stark focus: when you can't breathe (base layer of survival), nothing else matters. This means anything in a higher layer (i.e. fun, celebration of life, and inspiration) gets ignored. When we're gasping for air, that's our immediate priority. We can worry about fun once we can take a breath.

Maslow's model gives us a foundation for better understanding what truly drives individuals, ourselves included.

However, how do we truly know if our needs have been met?

NOTHING MORE THAN FEELINGS

Feelings are beacons indicating whether our needs are being met.

Yikes! I know, I know. Many don't want to discuss feelings. The word itself makes you cringe. (Ironically, because of your feelings.) Many of us were brought up with our parents telling us that we needed to control our emotions. Since many of us were left to our own devices after "use your words", we have a limited feelings vocabulary. Childhood peers rewarded us (or at least left us alone) for being tough. Workplaces discourage open displays of emotion.

To those who cringe at "feelings", it doesn't matter how much we ignore, deny, or repress them, because all humans have them. I'm not suggesting we dwell in them. This isn't a sharing circle or primal scream therapy. I'm talking about taking note of our feelings and letting them guide us as to which needs are being met and which ones are not.

On the basic level, we feel good when our needs are met and bad when they aren't. I like to call this the "Yum/Yuk Factor". We feel "Yum" when needs are met and "Yuk" when they are not.

Unless you are a heartless tin man, this binary view of feelings is a lousy pointer to WHAT needs are or are not being met. On the other end of the spectrum, it is an understatement to say that feelings are a topic that could fill another entire book. This topic could fill a complete library. If we searched for nonfiction titles about feelings, Amazon.com would list more than a million books.

For our purposes, we need a happy medium: A wide, but manageable, selection of well-known feelings that help point us to the most common human needs that need addressing.

This still almost sounds like an easy-to-use equation, doesn't it? Detect or observe an emotion in yourself or someone else, pick the emotion from the Yum/Yuk circles, then connect those feelings back to Maslow's Hierarchy, and, voila, instant analysis leading to conflict resolution.

THE SPRING DUCK THOUGHT EXPERIMENT

Though we can certainly use the circles and Hierarchy as guides, people aren't really that simple. Individuals are often driven by conflicting feelings. Two different people may have different feelings about the same needs. Even more complex, a single individual may have different feelings about the same needs at different times.

Have you ever ridden a playground spring duck? There are also horses, seals, and cartoon cars. If not, I guarantee there is one on a playground nearby. Straddle it like a horse and bend that spring in any direction. CAUTION: These are engineered for kids. Mind your head as an adult. You'll bend that spring all the way down.

Let's take two different individuals and put them on ducks: Amanda and Casey.

Casey is a thrill seeker. He likes hang gliding and scuba diving. The bigger the risk, the happier it makes him. On the duck, his need is for adventure (Self-Actualization on Maslow's Hierarchy). He loves the way he can bend the duck until his forehead touches the ground. He bounces up, then goes over backwards until his hair sweeps the ground. We can pick his feelings right off the Yum word cloud: Exhilarated, confident, and thrilled, to name a few.

Amanda likes stability and predictability. She likes spreadsheets and reads the manuals that come with her appliances so that she knows how to operate them safely and efficiently. The more she knows about what's coming next, the happier it makes her. On the duck, her need is for stability (Safety on Maslow's Hierarchy). She HATES the way the duck bends toward the ground, regardless of which direction it goes. We can pick her feelings about this off the Yuk chart: Aggravated, apprehensive, and worried. When the duck springs back so that she's upright again, her feelings appear on the Yum chart: Thankful.

Two different people experience the same exact spring duck. However, because their needs related to the situation are different, their feelings in the situation are also very different.

You're probably having some feelings of your own right now. What the heck am I supposed to do with this, Martin? If everything's constantly changing, what good is defining needs and feelings in the first place?

Believe me, I would love nothing better than to have a chart that told me exactly which feelings indicated which needs. That would make marriage, raising children, and work at the office all that much easier.

On the other hand, that would make us robots. The seemingly random nature of feelings and needs are what make us human in the first place.

Even though needs and feelings are elusive, there is undeniable value in being able to identify feelings and undersand they are connected to needs. The Curiosity Theory is not about head-shrinking. We're not attempting to analyze and figure people out. In fact, that would drive others away.

The Curiosity Theory is about making human connections. There are no hard answers here. Understanding that people's feelings point back to needs helps you sort through those feelings.

If I feel upset, that upset is pointing back to a need. Rather than dwell on the fact that I'm upset, asking Curious questions can help me identify my need(s):

Am I tired? (Base-level need.)

Am I in danger? (Safety-level need.)

Am I feeling left out? (Love/belonging-level need.)

Am I feeling incapable? (Esteem-lev`el need.)

Am I feeling uninspired? (Self-actualization-level need.)

To do this well does require some common sense. Certain feelings and needs just make sense together. Upset-related feelings make sense connected with hunger. Fear-related needs do not.

There is an important bottom line: It's not about being precise. it's about opening the conversation with someone (or yourself).

That's exactly how Yvette and I discovered a common goal by remaining curious when discussing camping. We both wanted to share with our boys a unique experience we had growing up.

I was all about excitement and glee at the idea of family camping trips (Yum!). Yvette showed signs of discomfort at the suggestion. She pulled back on the couch, almost like a slow-motion withdrawl from the conversation (Yuk!).

We both had to remain curious: What need had caused her reaction?

"It looks like camping might not be on your list," I asked. "I'm curious. Is there anything specific you dislike about it or is it just camping in general?"

She thought for a moment.

"I don't like sleeping outside," she said. "I like clean sheets, a soft mattress, and being able to take a hot shower before going to sleep."

Applying curiousity thorugh the structure of Feelings and Needs is how we found the solution that worked for everyone. We got to camp as a family. The boys and I got to swim in the lake and sleep under the stars. Yvette got her bed and a shower and everyone got hot coffee in the morning!

CHAPTER 5

HOW DO I BE CURIOUS?

One afternoon after I finished a workshop, Cheryl, one of the attendees, handed me an Office Depot box of rubber bands.

"Rubber bands are how I became curious," she said.

"Now I'm curious," I said. "How did rubber bands make YOU curious?"

"After years of trying to quit smoking, a friend introduced me to the technique of wearing a rubber band around my wrist," she said. "Each time I craved a cigarette, I would snap the rubber band."

"Didn't that hurt?" I asked.

"Yes," she said. "But it was only a 'minor' pain and it didn't cause any damage. Instead, that tiny snap would refocus me on why I was quitting: my husband, my kids, and my future plans. It worked. I haven't smoked in nearly ten years."

"Congratulations!" I said. "I'm wondering... how does that connect you to curiosity?"

She laughed.

"When I first took your class a couple years ago, I LOVED The Curiosity Theory concept," she said. "But I struggled to actually BE curious when it mattered. I had Curiosity all teed up. I PROMISED myself I'd be curious when conflict reared its ugly head. But I failed."

"Please, go on," I said, hooked.

"Well, I kept getting into arguments with my husband," she said. "I tried and tried to be curious, but when things got heated, I failed."

"But that's okay," I said. "It's human. Curiosity takes practice and I think you're on the right track."

She positively beamed.

"Yes!" she said. "But I did it with rubber bands! During an argument with my husband, I shouted, 'I SWEAR I'M BEING CURIOUS, BUT IT'S NOT WORKING!'"

"That was such a weird thing to say, we both laughed," she said. "It ended the argument. Then I explained The Curiosity Theory to him; how hard I was trying. He said, 'you haven't smoked in years; why not do the rubber band thing for this?'"

She raised her arm to show me a well-worn rubber band. Green, just like the ones in the box.

"For months, every time I felt conflict, I'd snap it," she said. "Now, I find myself reaching for it even before I'm aware there's conflict. It diverts my attention…"

She hesitated.

"Now, when I reach for it, I remember to be curious," she whispered. "I don't even snap it. I just ask a question."

Cheryl's not the first, nor will she be the last, to grapple with this element in The Curiosity Theory. She found the rubber band snap on her own. It worked for her.

I've heard innumerable versions of this kind of technique. Some people realize they're getting angry and count back from 10. Some practice "laughter therapy" and try to find humor in the moment of conflict. Others tell me of all kinds of breathing exercises—nose-only breathing, "square" breathing, yoga breathing. There are mantras and affirmations.

By all means, if you have something that works, use it. It could be a powerful stepping-stone to being consciously curious.

However, keep in mind that The Curiosity Theory is a mindset—a practice—not a quick fix. You don't apply it at the moment of crisis. You apply it all the time.

An instance of conflict is composed of several moments. They are gradual, so it's difficult to pinpoint them exactly. Much like the volume knob on our car radio, there are perfect graduations, but thresholds where we feel things are inaudible, loud enough, and too loud. These thresholds are different for each passenger.

It helps to look at the Timeline of a Conflict.

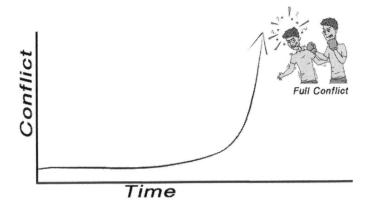

1. Moment of Recognition – When we notice that upset is happening, in ourselves or the others involved. Feelings are our indicator, and often start so subtly that nobody notices until the Reptilian Brain is taking over the interaction. The more practice we have with The Curiosity Theory, the sooner we can take advantage of The Opportunity of Curiosity.

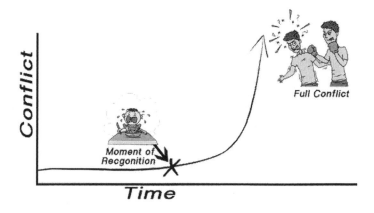

2. Window of Curiosity – That time between sensing oncoming upset and Reptilian Brain takeover. Ideally, this is where we make The Curiosity Theory inquiries to sooth the Reptilian Brain, create connections, and turn the conversation toward productive ends.

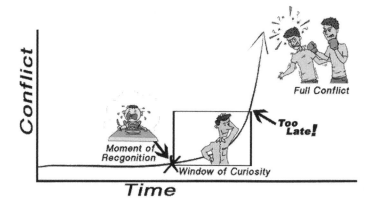

3. Moment of (hopefully, Avoided) Conflict – The point at which the Reptile Brain takes over. If we missed the Opportunity of Curiosity, this is the point at which an argument ensues.

It is important to be curious BEFORE the flash-point of conflict takes place. This means we have to already have a curious mindset. This takes practice. But each attempt gets us closer to truly being curious.

At this point in the conversation, [students] invariably ask me what kind of curious questions they should ask. They always want a "magic bullet" question. One that works every time.

So, in our conversation about the rubber band trick, I asked Cheryl:

"What kind of curious question do you ask?"

"It doesn't matter," she said. "I find any question works. Just the fact that I'm really, truly asking does the job."

I hate to sound like I'm trying to be Zen, but Curiosity is a mindset, not a question. It is a desire to truly connect with the other person.

If we must have questions, I suggest the journalist's checklist: Who? What? Where? When? Why? How?

Truth is, we won't eliminate the tension every time. People—including you and me—take time to shift gears, particularly when they're becoming upset. It's very likely there will still be a tense conversation, but the tension will even out and subside when everyone senses that someone is listening. That is the magic in curiosity. Our Curious mindset—not the question we are asking—is the magic bullet.

My personal style is to open with the statement, "I'm curious…".

I like to let it hang there for a moment: "I'm curious…"

That moment shifts the conversational dynamic just enough. This is the breather that gives us time to think; to stay calm. Often, this gives us time to think of the actual question.

The specific question being asked after that doesn't matter. Just open the dialogue.

CHAPTER 6

KNOW THYSELF

As water to a fish
As air to a bird
So is man to himself
~ Chinese Proverb

Warning #1: Please don't run around aiming The Curiosity Theory at everyone else. It's not a weapon or "tool" to be used to win arguments. If we use it this way we will often create a rift rather than a connection. We might hear, "Stop shrinking me!" and get waved off with, "Your Jedi Mind Tricks won't work on me, young Padawan."

The first person to be curious about is yourself.

I don't think I can emphasize that point enough: The Curiosity Theory is useless unless we are first curious about our own observations, feelings and needs.

Remember how our brain's structure echoes the development from primitive, Reptile Brain, to Higher-Brain? The highest level of Higher Brain allows us to have feelings about our own feelings.

That's where it starts.

This is not new knowledge. No less than Socrates--Greek philosopher and one of the founders of Western thinking--believed that the root of all knowledge was first knowing oneself. The same philosophical foundation appears in ancient Egyptian and Hindu thinking. It is ancient wisdom we modern humans are wise to heed.

Socrates also said, "Wisdom begins with wonder."

Sounds a lot like Curiosity, doesn't it.

This is not to say that applying The Curiosity Theory to ourselves is easy. Quite the contrary. In fact, I believe one of Socrates' Greek philosopher predecessors, Thales, nailed it, when he was asked, "What is the most difficult thing?"

"To know thyself," he said.

Then he was asked what was easiest.

"To give advice," he responded.

Applying The Curiosity Theory to ourself is true mindfulness.

I have a love-hate relationship with the word mindfulness. That poor word gets abused in the self-help world. It has become shorthand for believing that veganism, yoga, or meditating on a mountaintop will save the world. I'm not going there.

However, I love the technical definition:

> Mindfulness – the intentional, accepting and non-judgmental focus of one's attention on the emotions, thoughts and sensations occurring in the present moment.

It's about being aware of **ourselves** and our emotions and reactions in response to the moment; being able to navigate how we feel about how we feel.

Others respond to this, too. There is nothing quite as disarming as when we demonstrate our own humility to others; when they—and their Amygdales (Reptile brain)—sense that we are non-threatening.

By definition, if we are involved in a conflict, we are a significant part of that conflict. We are not passive. The conflict is not happening to us. This does NOT mean that anyone in the conflict is to blame. It DOES suggest that everyone involved has the ability to affect the outcome of that conflict.

We also have the ability to recall past conflicts, review them, and explore alternative scenarios and outcomes.

In getting to know ourselves, our own past is the first place to begin applying The Curiosity Theory. We are human. Our lives involve navigating conflict after conflict, whether with family, significant others, in the workplace, or in the schoolyard. Our memories are a ripe database of conflicts. Just as I was able to find instances where I (accidentally) encountered curiosity disrupting the pattern of conflict, others will be able to find those instances in their own life.

Caution: Before you start rooting around your psyche, make sure that you are not seeking to dwell. Though it can feel therapeutic, this exercise is not intended as a way to solve past relationship issues, which often have more complicated root causes than just one or a few conflicts. It may be enlightening to explore a past relationship through this [visualization exercise], but our intent is to focus on a moment of conflict.

Now, take a moment to relax. Sit back. Close your eyes. Slow your breathing.

I want you to recall an argument.

Remember the person you were with.

Remember the topic.

Remember the words.

Remember the other person's reactions.

See if you can bring back the feelings you had at that moment.

CAREFUL; DON'T DWELL: Be kind. Forgive yourself if you got it wrong. For example, if you reacted badly or if you are feeling guilty for anger. Let go of those feelings, as well as any anger or concern toward the other person. This exercise isn't about regrets. If anything, let those feelings inform our future selves to prepare for how to handle conflict differently next time.

Now, given your knowledge of feelings and needs from chapter 4, can you identify your feelings related to this argument?

Now be curious:

What were your needs?

What were your feelings?

Keep visualizing: Based on your new knowledge of those needs, what would you do differently if you were currently in this same conflict?

Feeling	Need	Different Action

With the different action, how does the scenario change?

Using The Curiosity Theory, what questions could we ask that would break that conflict in the moment?

Try this exercise with a few different arguments. Make an effort to revisit conflicts with at least three different individuals, so as not to get in a rut of trying to analyze the same person repeatedly.

TAKE NOTE: Is there anything common across these visualizations? Are there any patterns in the reaction in each scenario?

Feeling	Need	Do differently

When we see a way to better engage others in the future we know we now have a higher level of self-awareness.

When we consciously begin making that change, we change the outcome of any conflict.

Welcome to wisdom.

CHAPTER 7

CONCLUSION

The romantic comedy, *You've Got Mail,* starring Tom Hanks and Meg Ryan is one of my favorite films with a poignant Curiosity Theory moment.

Two bookstore owners—Ryan, with a tiny neighborhood shop, and Hanks, opening a neighborhood-shop-killing mega store next door (think Barnes & Nobel)—are unknowingly in a romance with each other conducted anonymously via an online chat. Their battle in the real world, with the comedy-of-errors, is the gradual suspicion and then realization that they actually adore and are perfect for each other.

Hanks' seemingly impersonal, corporate business manner infuriates Ryan at every turn. Endlessly polite, she confides to her BFF a secret desire to let her anger fly and just scream, yell, hit, kick, and bite.

We've all been there, right?

When the online and offline plot lines collide, she lets it all fly in an epic rant, punctuated by tears and couch-cushion punches.

"I don't understand why you are so upset. It's just business; it's not personal," says Hanks. [paraphrased line]

"It's always personal to somebody," Ryan sniffles. [real line]

She has a point.

But she also feels empty. Though it felt good in the moment, her rant failed to have the results she had hoped. It left her feeling awkward and empty. It shoved Hanks away, which was the opposite of what she really wanted.

"Now, was that everything you wanted it to be?" asks Hanks.

No. He doesn't actually ask that. It's me. Every time I see this film, I want to reach through the screen, grab Ryan and Hanks like a ventriloquist's dummies, and change their conversation.

Better yet, I want to introduce the characters to The Curiosity Theory. They're so very human; just like you and me.

"What are your feelings?" I'd ask. "Follow them to your needs. Do you need to be understood? Respected? Appreciated?"

I began this book--and my personal exploration of The Curiosity Theory—with accidents pointing toward something I sought: as a means of turning conflict into constructive interaction. This includes more productive professional relationships, stronger friendships, and closer family ties.

Most likely, the little that I have included—curiosity, mindfulness, emotional intelligence, even Reptile Brain—is new to you. I have tried to keep my approach as common sense as possible.

I believe that many people already practice 80% of what I've discussed. However, I'd also wager that most do so accidentally and intermittently, at best. This is what I found in myself when I began to focus on The Curiosity Theory.

I hear my own journey echoed in the questions posed by coaching clients and seminar participants:

"What about when I slip and argue anyway?"

"What if I just want my way?"

What if being mad and right just feels good?"

"That would make you human," I answer. "I do it all the time."

We can choose to employ The Creativity Theory or not. Sometimes I'm just too tired. Sometimes I spoil myself in selfishness. Sometimes I just plain forgot to engage my curiosity.

Invariably, ranting, arguing, and fighting just feels good. There is even evidence showing that expressing pain and frustration by cussing actually relieves stress, lowers blood pressure, and helps us handle the moment. I know when I accidentally hit my thumb with a hammer, letting fly with a good expletive or two makes everything better. (That and seriously whacking the nail on the second try.)

I agree that "flipping the bird" to a driver who just cut you off satiates that Reptile Brain.

It often feels like we could win if we could just fight hard enough. If we could just assert enough of our logic that the other person would get it.

But what does it get you in the end? Worst case scenario is fired, divorced, punched, arrested, even shot. Best-case scenario is a moment's release, then emptiness or regret. Just like Meg Ryan's bookseller, now you have to undo the damage. Apologize. Grovel. Hand-write notes. Call the florist. Visit a divorce attorney.

We are left with the grand reveal: it's not about logic. It's not about control or overpowering the other person. Meg Ryan's bookseller will never be able to punch the couch cushion hard enough.

Why? Because it's about human nature and personal connection.

It takes effort—awareness, restraint—to stay cool and refrain from jumping into the fray, especially when others we are engaged with are diving right in; desperately trying to get us to engage.

Finally, with great effort comes great reward. We realize this at all levels. It can be the simple relief (in smell or nagging) we get from just taking out the trash when it's needed. At the grander end, it can be the satisfaction of closing a major sale or the hard-won accomplishment of earning another certification or diploma.

The Curiosity Theory is somewhere in the middle on that spectrum. It takes more effort than the trash; less than a whole degree.

It takes some study, a conscious effort, and real practice. But, the rewards my clients and I have realized far outweigh that effort.

Experience has revealed that those who get the most out of any self-help program are those willing to study it, explore it openly, experiment, practice, and make it their own.

Occasionally, a seminar skeptic poses the "Why would I lock myself into your philosophy?" question. There are many variations on this, summarized as:

"I have many choices in how to handle a conflict. Why would I choose The Curiosity Theory over others?"

You shouldn't. You should use the best tool for the job at hand.

I see The Conscious Curiosity not as a philosophy, but as one tool among many. In fact, I invite everyone to dive deeper by visiting some of my favorite resources, including *Emotional Intelligence* by Daniel Goleman, *Nonviolent Communication* by Marshall

B. Rosenberg, and *Conscious Choosing for Flow* by Hayden D.M. Hayden (my mentor and the inspiration for my own exploration of The Curiosity Theory).

The more we study, the more we know. The more tools we have at our disposal, the more prepared and adept we will be in our choice and the better able to employ The Curiosity Theory.

Finally, I want to invite you to check out my programs and seminars. I'd also like the opportunity to bring The Curiosity Theory to your organization or one of your events. To check my availability please visit me at www.TheCuriosityTheory.com or email me at martin@martinlopez.com. I am continuously researching and studying to keep The Curiosity Theory current and relevant. This book is the foundation of my programs and what I present.

One of the great joys of conducting seminars is that participants teach me as much as I teach them. I hear insights like Chery's curiosity-inducing rubber band snap or new examples of how someone got a promotion, grew their business, or enriched their family life by applying curiosity—accidentally or on purpose. After a morning's discussion and seminars, I find that I come away with as much insight and as many new ideas as those who came to learn from me.

In the end, we all depart richer for a little bit of curiosity.

Martin

ABOUT THE AUTHOR

Martin Lopez

A graduate of the University of Santa Monica's Spiritual Psychology program, Martin Lopez founded The Curiosity Theory with the mission of helping individuals and teams grow through [improved] communication and collaboration.

During his many years as a real estate professional and mortgage banker Martin observed innumerable opportunities lost due to misaligned conflict and self-sabotaging communications. Invariably, the issues were human rather than technical: simple misunderstandings, tragicomic disagreement, or fear-driven distrust.

Through long-term study with mentors and formal study programs, Martin sought to identify the human patterns common to these interpersonal breakdowns, as well as a methodology for disrupting those patterns. The Curiosity Theory is Martin's highly-accessible manual for this.

Martin travels extensively, sharing "The Curiosity Theory" with organizational and corporate audiences. He also teaches "Conscious Choosing for Flow" as an affiliate of Conscious Choosing, LLC.

THE CURIOSITY THEORY

The Curiosity Theory aligns itself with individuals committed to creating positive change in the world one shift at a time. Its guiding principles:

Mutual Respect

Mutual Purpose

Appreciation

Focus

Follow-Through

If your team or business struggles with a misalignment of competing visions, emotional reactivity, lack of follow through and not getting the results you need to be valuable and effective then our 1/2 Day program "The Curiosity Theory for Pros" or 2 Day Program "Conscious Choosing for Flow" are for you.

The Curiosity Theory for Pros & Conscious Choosing for Flow

What if... you could learn a simple, tired and proven way of transforming the destructive tension of conflict into the dynamic energy of creativity on the spot, in real time, while addressing your needs, the needs of the team, and the customers all while creating a buy-in and sharing goals? How valuable would it be for you?

Martin's programs give you this empowering technology through a model called Skills for Living and the Formula for Flow.

Our Workshops are a combination of instruction, exercises and coaching that happens in the process of solving actual challenges and problems, in the moment, by ...

- Safely and respectfully addressing unique problems and issues.

- Identifying the root causes of conflict and not just the symptoms.

- Teaching skills that participants can use in all work and personal relationships.

- Developing leaders by providing a simple, consistent, tried and proven process.

And we do this in a single day.

For more information on our programs visit our website
www.TheCuriosityTheory.com

Too the best of my knowledge there are no perfect relationships, but there are perfect opportunities to practice human connection.

#StayCuriousMyFriend

NOTE

NOTE

NOTE

NOTE

NOTE

NOTE

Made in the USA
San Bernardino, CA
11 June 2016